Rescue from the dark

Paul Francis

Fair Acre Press

Fair Acre Press

First published in Great Britain in 2021 by Fair Acre Press
www.fairacrepress.co.uk

A CIP catalogue record for this book is available
from the British Library

ISBN 978-1-911048-52-7

Typeset by Nadia Kingsley
Cover design by Nadia Kingsley

Acknowledgements

Special Offer – first prize in the Scottish Huntington's Disease Association's poetry competition, 2018.

On the Edge – shortlisted, Welshpool poetry competition, 2018.

Ballad of Paulette Wilson – published in Black Lives Matter, 2020.

Clocking Off – published in Bread and Roses poetry award, 2020.

There and Back – third prize, Crewe Writers' competition, 2020.

Short-term Investment – second prize, Beyond the Storm, 2020.

About Paul Francis

Paul Francis is a retired teacher, living in Much Wenlock. He is a versatile writer who has won two national play-writing competitions, as well as publishing a novel and an autobiography. He has written extensively on education, and has been a prolific writer of materials for secondary school pupils.

In poetry, he has won three national poetry competitions, and been placed (second or third) in three others. He is active in the West Midlands poetry scene, regularly reading at a wide variety of venues, and he was poet in residence at the Wenlock Poetry Festival, 2016. In 2020 he wrote a sonnet a day during lockdown, published on his website www.paulfranciswrites.co.uk, and subsequently as *Turning Off the News* (2020).

Previous Publications

His main poetry collections, published by Liberty Books, are:

Various Forms (2010)

5-string Banjo (2016)

Sonnets with Notes (2019)

He has also published a series of topical pamphlets, the latest of which is *Dreams of Brexit*, to be published in Spring 2021.

Contents

Rescue	9
Betrayal	10
Dover Beach, June 2016	12
A chat with Clem in 1951	14
Winter	16
Ecosystem	17
Special Offer	18
Testimony	19
Fit for Purpose?	20
Frances at Nashoba	22
On the Edge	24
Living in Limbo	26
The Ballad of Paulette Wilson	28
The Idea of the Garden	30
Funny Girl	32
A Class Act	34
Oaks	35
Dominic Cummings Explains:	36
Clocking Off	38
Sir Arthur Conan Doyle	40
Fatal Attraction	41
Man to Man	42
Mentor	43
Working with Water	44
To Hell and Back	46
Odyssey	48
A Lesson from Auschwitz	50
Syrian Feast	51
The Lighthouse, Wolverhampton	52
Delroy's Path	54
The Ballad of Tracy Rogers	56

Woke?   59
Homeless at Christmas   60
There and Back   62
Return to Work   64
Short-term Investment   65
Hippocrates at Wuhan   66
The other virus   67
Liberation   68
Freedom Fighter   70
Leavers   71
Armour   72
Step back   74
Pick-me-up: 75

Notes   *77*

Rescue

Gently, as if he were an injured child,
Patrick scoops up this isolated man
and carries him to safety, while his friends
(a rugby pack who've planned a line-out move)
provide protection, give him breathing space.
No time to think. Do what you've got to do.
The man they save is racist, white but this
is no self-sacrifice. *It's not for him.*
We did it for our kids. We leave him there
he dies, and we know what the judge will say.
Some black boys kill a white man, no-one cares
about what happened first. They think ahead
for others; they take action, as a team.
Police do that, and George Floyd's still alive.

Betrayal

The way it's supposed to work is this:
she goes into the trenches, fights disease
and thanks to her and others folk get well.
This isn't Disney. There are some they lose.
The odds are, mostly, reasonable.
She goes back, knackered, to the flat
where, with her mates (both doctors) they relax,
share drinks, swap jokes and celebrate
the buzz of doing something that's worthwhile.

But now, this bastard screws up everything.
The shifts get longer, and the odds get worse.
More people die. More conversations
telling the relatives their loved one's gone
and no, they cannot see them, say goodbye.
There's not the time, the beds, the kit they need.
Those rules about the way they're supposed to work:
protection? safety stuff? They've been ripped up.
On top of that, she isn't feeling well.

She hasn't got a fever or a cough.
She's told they can't arrange a swab
so she should stay at work. She's changed.
She's not a fighter, she's become
a double agent, nibbling away –
pass on the guilt, contaminate the team.
But getting someone else to swab her throat
puts them at risk. She breaks the rules,
cuts corners, swabs herself.

It comes back positive. That much is clear:
stay home and sit it out for fourteen days.
Her name comes off the list. The pressure grows
on those who still clock in. Odds? Even worse.
Her mates must stay at home. So, worse again.
The symptoms aren't the start. Before she knew
who has she passed this on to? Who might die?
Where did she get it? Was it her mistake?
When will the questions end?

Dover Beach, June 2016

The sea is calm tonight
a placid moat, which wasn't there
ten thousand years ago. Beneath these tides
a bridge to Europe sank from sight.
We wiped that from our memories.

So now we toss for it, leave or remain.
The money men are confident.
The sums, the experts all add up
one way. They smile, shake hands, assure
the people down below it's all quite clear.

They get the finger. Those below
are savouring an unaccustomed taste.
Power. Routinely, they're not heard
their ballot papers are ignored, but now
their votes will count.

They're reaching for a land of dreams,
so various, so beautiful, so new.
The promise is, they will take back control,
an end to shadows slipping through the net,
to values, habits being undermined.

Analysts grimly calculate
the consequence: the fresh uncertainty,
postponement, haggle, compromise,
the moat collapsing, being drained...
but sod analysis. Just vote.

Which leaves me, one more loner on the beach.
I'm fine. The house and garden, pension paid
but there's the grandkids. What's their legacy?
I want for them my early land of dreams –
the job, the home, the planet that still works...

Ignorant armies, and confused alarms.
I listen to the shingle suck and slide
the wash of rancour, easy answers, lies
and wait for morning when the coin comes down –
a stumble or a leap into the dark.

A chat with Clem in 1951

Traffic was slower, thinner then
but the smog was extra thick.
He's on the pavement. Still looks slightly dazed
so this could be my chance.

"Mr. Attlee, could I have a word?"
I lost. Mr. Churchill, surely, will oblige…
"I need to talk to you. Because you lost."
That gets him. Mustn't let him slip away.
"You got more votes than Labour's ever got."
It's not the votes. You have to win the seats.
"After all you've done –"
We did what must be done. We can be proud,
whether or not we stay in power.
"And why do you think you lost?"
We're deep in debt, depend on aid.
The Labour Party's split, austerity…
"But just six years ago –"
We won. And that was a surprise.
"To you?"
To everyone. Nearly four hundred seats.
The Manchester Guardian doubted if we'd win.
"And you beat Churchill. Why do you think that was?"
He said we'd have to take Gestapo powers.
That's nasty talk. Voters don't go for that.
"They don't?"
Their whole campaign was Churchill. Nothing else.
People don't like to back a one-man band.
"I'll make a note of that. In those six years –"
After the war they wanted, needed change.
A welfare system, cradle to the grave.

"Your childhood. Comfortable?"
It was. But as a lad I volunteered
in the East End. I saw what poverty
could do to families. Never forgotten that.
"Housing, social security and health.
You gave them that, and now they've turned you out."
They have the vote. It must be theirs to use.
"And you're not bitter? Angry? Feel betrayed?"
Would it be helpful if I were?
"Your legacy. What Churchill said."
"Sheep in sheep's clothing"? Doesn't bother me.
"A modest man, with much to be modest about?"
He claims that wasn't him.
And we worked well together, in the war.
"You oiled the wheels, you calmed them down.
You built a structure in which he could thrive."
I said, we worked together well.
"And what's your view of leadership?"
It's not Olivier ranting at the troops.
More like the chairman of the board. You need
an overview, see how the jigsaw fits.
"And if the pieces won't go where they're put?"
That's when it's time to go. As I must now.

He crosses to his car, exchanges smiles
with the woman in the driver's seat.
She finishes the row she's on
then puts her knitting down.

Winter

after Brueghel

Aloof, they guard their branches, sitting still
while one eccentric flies. Who'd be a rook?
But if, like them, you perch upon this hill
you see for miles across the whiteness. Look
in the distance at the sharpened peaks that break
this chill horizon. Lower down, the trees
pace out in lines, down to the lake
the core and basic on the town. You freeze
unless you're moving. Stoke the fire's glow
or chase the kids across the ice; join men who stand
in groups, watch lovers, hand in frozen hand,
crunching across the January snow
as hunters head for home, stride after stride.
The dogs have had enough. Get back inside.

Ecosystem

Like cartoon villains, through the piles of waste
the hooked bills rip their systematic way.
We watch the vultures' cleaning with distaste
and miss the deadlier pattern of decay.
The livestock that they scavenge have been fed
with chemicals, so when the scouring's done
the scourers die, offstage. Meanwhile the dead
they would have cleaned lie rotting in the sun.
The Parsee funerals, burials in the sky
where bodies are not burnt but eaten clean
depend upon the vultures. Far too late
the outcasts are the chosen, as they try
to breed more vultures. On the carrion scene
a million microbes breathe again, and wait.

Special Offer

The commercial you are watching –
don't change the channel, please –
will illustrate the features
of Huntington's disease.
Our product's unobtrusive.
You may not see a sign
but once we start that's twenty years'
inexorable decline.
Your mum seems strangely lazy,
your husband's in a mood,
your grandma's having trouble
in managing her food.
The symptoms of frustration
are hardly to be borne
until your prayers are answered
and all feeling is withdrawn.
It's a deadly diagnosis –
who wants to face the worst?
Some seem to live in ignorance,
some realise they're cursed.
But that's the choice we offer.
We think we're here to stay
so – will you look us in the eye
or will you turn away?

Testimony

Next up, council surveyor, who should check
that building meets the regs. Grenfell was his –
passed on because a senior guy had left.
That's one of ten. Two hundred and thirty years'
of knowhow – swapped for a fresh graduate.
He'd had three people's work dropped in his lap.
A hundred and thirty projects at a time
and *No, I wasn't totally au fait*
with all the details, specs and articles…
Went in at weekends, lay awake at night.
Didn't complain. They wouldn't want to know.
He had resigned before the fire, because
he couldn't do his job. *Before those cuts…*
… so many lives… He finishes in tears.

Fit for Purpose?

A home for everyone? That scheme
became a luxury, a dream.
Since then we've had a change of mind
and social housing's left behind.
We're after profit now, full speed.
Those we don't want on land we need
get shifted out to miles away –
we lose the ones on lower pay.
Refurbishment, exclusive deals,
a transformation that appeals
to more upmarket tenants, who
demand a smarter, cleaner view.
Inspection's privatised, and cheap.
Their survey, quick and not that deep
declared an eyesore, understand?
Plus, cheaper cladding saved five grand.
Councillors tried to raise concerns
but we ignore a worm that turns.
We don't explain, we don't resign –
what matters is the bottom line.

Now there's this fire. The mood is mean
because we're nowhere to be seen.
We're stuck. Our legal team advise
that saying nothing would be wise.
Stay put and lock your door, we'd said;
the structure means the fire won't spread.
Except, that small cosmetic change
we made contrived to rearrange
the building's make-up; now the fire
leaps up the tower, higher, higher…
A new agenda. Different rules.
Survivors, funerals and schools.
Sort out donations? Calm their fears?
Co-ordinate the volunteers?
Demands and questions run berserk
with doubt – how can we make this work?
Out in the street we get that stare:
that we don't know and we don't care.
Us, find solutions? Not a hope.
They know – we know – that we can't cope.

Frances at Nashoba

Just her, and this young carpenter.
They're all that's left behind
now that the commune's sunk into the mud.
No need for enemies to light the fires
or throw the stones they used
to terrorise the crowds. At five feet ten,
Scots brogue and flaming hair,
a million minds stored memories
of seeing Frances Wright.

The carpenter's surprised. He'd heard
the stories, feared the worst, assumed
she'd interfere, or criticise his work.
But no. She sits him down, insists
he shares her meal, talks of workers' rights,
how bad she is at housework, all the stuff
that's rolling through her head.
He loves to hear her talk.

Compared with other wives, she was prepared.
She'd fought for birth control,
divorce and married women's property.
So when she finds a husband, sees him change
into a bully who declares she's lost her mind
she's not surprised she has to fight.
She has matured, but to the world she's still
the Scarlet Harlot, Whore of Babylon.

It was a tempting dream. New Harmony
had seemed so possible, the union
of work and care, the heaven on earth
where every member's valued properly.
She'd backed herself, rode forty miles a day.
Her slaves would be redeemed, would earn
their freedom on this frontier, this swamp
she thought she'd civilise. Hope slipped away
as time, mosquitoes, death sat smiling by.

On the Edge

Bright summer days, as lads
they'd clamber, dangle down
bouncing against the cliff in search of eggs
life hanging by a thread.
It's work for men, all weathers, now.
The appetite for Whitby Jet
is endless, fuelled by the Queen's
unvarying ensemble, black and grey.

A stick of dynamite can blast
the jet out from a face
smash it to smithereens.
Jet heals the toothache, eases labour pains
but when that stick is lit and doesn't blow
whose job is it to go and check it out?
It's deadly work, is mining jet,
and there's no cure for that.

A miner in a tunnel, bent below,
knows that the tons of rock and earth
can snuff him out at any time they choose.
Easy to believe, deep in the dark,
that jet has power to drive the serpents back,
ward off the spirits lurking down below.
When he gets home he'll keep the kiddies safe;
ebony fire, nailed to a post.

They get it to the workshop. Still not safe.
A casual match, dropped on a dusty floor,
can seem extinguished, then erupt in flame.
A lazy workman with a high-speed drill
can splinter five hours' labour in a flash.
But then you look in the museum
at what those prehistoric craftsmen made,
marvels they fashioned with the simplest tools.

The tide of trade ebbed out, then in.
For years, the exports fed a frenzied boom
until the cheaper imports hit the dock.
Young men, ambitious for a rapid rise,
dismissed apprenticeships. Too long to wait.
The killer was the deadly wheel of taste
as younger, brighter women dared defy
the monochrome of widowhood.

Living in Limbo

They fight for places on the boat, relieved
until the water level starts to rise.
The captain talks of going back. No way.
Keep baling, plug the hole, and bale again.

A ship appears, a dim light in the dark
just as the boat capsizes. Holding on,
gripping a spar of wood, scarred by its nails
but letting go would finish everything.

The wave of kindness washes over him.
Packets of food, a cool refreshing hose
and maybe this is how the chapter ends.
Dry land, clean clothes, a fresh new page.

Australia has a cordon sanitaire,
its sheath an archipelago
of islands, like a filter trapping dirt,
where possible pollutants are detained.

The foreigners are parked inside a cage,
issued with flip flops, left to wait and sweat.
Regional Processing Centre, says the sign,
but **Manus Prison** is the phrase he'll use.

The aim is cut them off. No pens. No pads.
Starve them of hope, they'll beg to be sent back.
Conditions need to be intolerable;
staff whistleblowers get two years in jail.

Inside his mattress, Behrouz hides a phone.
He sends his friends these surreptitious texts
that build into a book that wins a prize –
a pebble that's a ripple, then a wave.

But six years on, he's still there, doing time.
Sat on a roof, and smoking, late at night.
Intelligence surrounded by the dark
an island that refuses to be drowned.

The Ballad of Paulette Wilson

The UK has a cancer which is gnawing at its heart –
the cancer's name is Brexit and it's tearing us apart.
More money for the NHS? No, that was just a laugh;
they're breaking up the service as they terrorise the staff.
Home Office gets the message. The verdict's all too clear:
if you weren't born in Britain, then they don't want you here.
They're not planning for the future with a rational campaign;
they're rounding up the foreigners to put them on a plane.

They pick on Paulette Wilson, down Wolverhampton way,
who gets the dreaded letter that says she cannot stay.
She came here from Jamaica when she was ten years old.
But now she is a granny, and they've put her life on hold.
Hostile Environment's the plan. It's magic: "Just like that!"
She's always paid her taxes but – shazam! – she's lost her flat.
She spends a week at Yarl's Wood. They send her to Heathrow.
They don't care what she says to them, they mean to make her go.

Her daughter works her socks off, her MP fights the case.
The Home Office is clinging on, they're scared of losing face.
The Guardian writes her story, their readers send support;
solicitors are sure this case will not stand up in court.
She gets a gala evening and a cheque for half a grand
from a load of local poets and a ukulele band.
Eventually the pressure tells, the scandal is a stain
and Paulette gets good news at last – permission to remain.

She wasn't looking for revenge. What mattered to Paulette
was that they say they're sorry, that they viewed this with regret.
Now that this scandal's in the news, they'll want the slate wiped clean.
She used to work in Parliament with staff from the canteen
but suddenly she's back there, on Tuesday, first of May,
where Caroline Nokes, Home Office, has stuff she needs to say:
"To Mrs. Wilson, specially…" – she looks her in the eyes –
"You suffered from our policies. I must apologise."

Recommendations were ignored. So many people wait
for compensation that is due; for Paulette it's too late.
She was bright and energetic but they tore her life apart
and now, at 64, she's died. The battle broke her heart.
She gets a Covid funeral, just twenty folk inside
but there's hundreds in the car park, they're applauding her with pride.
When governments abuse their power, we have to set them right
and she's the Windrush champion who has taught us how to fight.

The Idea of the Garden
for Katherine Swift

The garden starts in winter
in her head. It grows alarmingly.
Outside, the grey December gloom
can't dull her technicolour dreams.
Just like the monks
she will grow flowers and herbs,
the fruit and vegetables, the crops she needs.
She has a sense, but cannot draw the plan,
provide a model, demonstrate.
All that she has are words, and
what she has conceived.

For this is garden as encyclopaedia.
In this one plot
she'll tell the stories of the gardens that have been
from Alfred's time to now.
She will have box that Romans loved,
wild daffodils from medieval tapestries,
the lavender and rosemary
brought here by Norman monks.
The cloister arches borrowed from the church,
the pears from seventeenth century German,
alongside flowers from painting by the Dutch.
Knot gardens that Elizabeth the First
would surely recognise.

She does not own the land.
She's not done this before.
How much will all this cost?
Where can she look for help?
So much she does not know –
so much that could go wrong
that others might not like
but still: the germ of it is there.

Wind whistles under doors
hunting for doubt, for weakening resolve
but still this infant concept
is nestling in her head.
She hugs it, tight and warm,
and urges it to grow.

Funny Girl

for Jacky Fleming

I stomp the treadmill
looking for a laugh.
Sucking the pencil
gazing at the sky.
What if they never, ever
laugh again?

The books sold well
so they are out of print.
The reputation's there, the memories
but that's not revenue.
The money men have left the books behind
measured the bottom line
moved on.

I push myself.
Give up a glorious afternoon
seek out some bookshop miles away
deep in the Shropshire wilds.
A two hour shift:
smile and pen for hire
looking for passing trade.

She takes me by surprise.
I was prepared for grateful feminists,
for clear-eyed daughters
who have learned through my cartoons
the facts of sex, of men.

So, stooping, fragile,
walking with a stick
apologising that she's bought no book
why does she climb these stairs?

Her daughter died of cancer
hard and slow.
Kept on her dressing table
wedged against the glass
my drawing of a bolshie little girl
who won't accept defeat, the world.

That's how she lived
while time allowed
and on the order for her funeral
the little girl lives on.
Never give up.

A Class Act

No question, it's subversive. Hear those screams
slice through the gallery. The silence rules
are shredded, as the playground blasts your ears –
the cry of children finding something new.
A zoo within a hangar. Round the walls
are grids of photographs, three thousand schools.
A template – camera distance, rows – does not impose
dulled uniformity. Each character appears
anonymous, unique and undefined
by captions, categories, names. The face
is all we need. They look at us. Somehow
this rebel with Napoleonic dreams
has caught these kids and lured them to this place
which is their right. Our future, here and now.

Oaks

From far below we see them
fixed figures on the skyline
Indians in silhouette.

Midway, as we climb up
there's lines of other trees
in regimented rows.

But once we reach the top
there is no bottom line
no business plan.

Each oak decides
the way its dervish arms will twist
strikes its own attitude.

Inside, each statue teems with life –
a thousand different busy grubs
pursue their diet, and their dreams.

Dominic Cummings Explains:
how we brought the symptoms from London to Durham and back

I'll do it myself, I don't trust Number Ten
there's no way I'm having them cock up again.
It's a breach of the lockdown, the press come in hard;
advisers are sure that my son's the trump card.
So this is the showdown, I shan't be a scruff;
white shirt with a collar, that should be enough.

I want to say sorry – but that's cos I'm late.
(I learnt from a diva who said 'Make 'em wait'.)
If you think I'll say sorry for what I have done
forget it. I am the inscrutable one
and here in the garden I'll give you a sight
of what how I was thinking and why I was right.

When Mary was ill my response was not slow.
No childcare in London. To Durham we'll go.
I drove like the clappers, no stops on the way
but with three separate houses there's somewhere to stay.
Observe isolation, the lock down applies
    – except for a short trip to test out my eyes.

The story of lockdown, so Mary reports,
is a Spectator article airing her thoughts.
She doesn't say Durham, the day trip's not there;
when threats are involved then you have to take care.
My argument's logical, nothing's amiss
and there's no consultation in any of this.

My agenda with Boris is full on these days.
Each morning I fix on the points I shall raise.
At the time he was ill so my problems could wait;
I thought that he'd got quite enough on his plate
and on deeper reflection it's simple to see
that the person best placed to decide this was me.

I recognise others might not think the same.
There's some who resigned, they accepted the blame
and they had no symptoms. The hacks want to know
if I'll be resigning. The answer is no.
I never considered it. I am the one
who took back control, and I got Brexit done.

There's families split who are going berserk
and scientists say that I've trashed all their work
'cos the test and trace system's dependent on trust.
They do what they can but I do what I must.
I don't want to hear about folk who might die.
I'm one in a million. The rules don't apply.

Clocking Off

Emmanuel doesn't feel right –
a fever, loss of appetite.
Not safe. He hears that warning voice
but knows he doesn't have a choice.
He's in his sixties. He came here
from Guinea Bissau, and it's clear
if you look up and you want more
you're starting at the bottom floor.

This central London tower block
has migrant cleaners, round the clock
reporting in – but no-one's there.
They're cleaning up, they're taking care
on every floor, of every room –
a spotless fourteen-story tomb.

Bosses insist things must be clean
but they're safe home in quarantine.
The civil servants on the staff
have read the figures, seen the graph.
No need for gestures or pretence –
staying at home is common sense.
But men from Pakistan, Brazil
are told to be there, feeling ill
as they negotiate around
the minefield of the underground.

Emmanuel keeps on clocking in
because the sick pay won't begin
to pay his bills. Ten quid an hour
is not much money, not much power
but things get worse the day he stops.
He'll keep on working till he drops.
You never get if you don't ask
but no, they won't give him a mask.
Five days, and all his worries cease.
Emmanuel Gomez, rest in peace.

Maybe, amidst the grief and fear
it's wrong to look for reasons here,
to seek some pattern we might see
in rampant inequality.
Why ask what purpose we might find
beneath the surface, out of mind?
OK, a virus ran berserk
but still, there's irony at work.
The role of this unhealthy site?
The Ministry of Justice, right?

Sir Arthur Conan Doyle

His son has gone. It's more than he can take.
It would make sense to lose him to the war
but to this foreign plague? What can he do?
No more detective tales. The pioneer
of rational deduction – not a clue.
He speaks to Cambridge scientists, who try
to keep straight faces as this famous name
insists that ectoplasm is the core
of all psychic phenomena. It's clear
he's lost it, but their parents are the same.
Distracted, distant, always asking why.
There's damage to the body and the mind,
all kinds of wreckage drifting in its wake,
the debris a pandemic leaves behind.

Fatal Attraction

Daniel, a Melbourne astrophysicist,
was keen on health and safety. "I propose:
wear a magnetic armband on your wrist.
You then insert two magnets in your nose
so when your hand gets too close to your face
alarms go off, and you'll be safe again."
One magnet in each nostril was in place
attached to ones outside his nose, but when
the outside ones came off, the inside pair
locked on each other. Daniel was surprised
but not dismayed. He brought the pliers to bear
and then he found that they got magnetised.
In hospital the diagnosis ran:
"self-isolation, boredom – and a man."

Man to Man

Maybe we should have had this chat before…
In an ideal world, I wouldn't tell you this,
you'd find it out yourself. You'd have the time
to work things out, in that secure cocoon:
state welfare, cradle to the grave, and grants;
a car and house that's better than your dad's;
a job for life, the pension, all the things
I shan't be passing on.
Don't get me wrong. You're doing fine.

Our sexist, racist hang-ups all got ditched –
you hardly skipped a beat. Technology
that baffles us does what you tell it to.
But power? No, you said, not interested
in aging men with empty words.
You didn't see them buy the right to rule,
rip up the rule-book. Health, elections, banks,
environment. They will not stop
until somebody stops them. Yes, that's you.

Your job. Your kids need breathing space
a future worth the wait, but time
is running out. We spent it, like the rest.
You need to know the all together dream
is not a dream. Pandemic brought it out
but cling on tight before they sell it off.
So here's your homework: solidarity.
It will be tough, you may not win
but that's the legacy.

Mentor

That was the day that set her on this road.
She's fifteen, walking to the old hotel
that this guy uses as his studio.
John's fifty-five. He's teaching her guitar
and right away he spots it. He can tell
scales aren't her thing. The repetition stuff
("Just do it, right?") is not where she belongs.
Write me a song, he says. *This week. It's fine
if you don't think it isn't good enough,
don't matter none. Just show me.* That's the code
she's waited for, the light she needs, although
she's just a kid. She has no clue how far
talent might take her. Five years down the line
she gets a job in Nashville, writing songs.

Working with Water

It's 101: New Settlement
where all you need is water, right?
The Moors have calculated that
the river Darro is four miles away.
That's close enough. They sketch their plan.

They will construct this liquid labyrinth
with links of channels running into tanks.
The top feeds off into the next link down
the sediment sinks slowly to the bed.
It's running, getting purer all the time...

There is a desert memory
of camels, miles of sand and thirst
where food is surplus, one more luxury
but water is the factor which decides
whether you live or die.

This palace is a different, distant world
that's rich in time, where standing in the wings
a cast of servants wait to meet all needs.
But in the fountains, basins, brimming bowls
that memory lives on.

A chain of courtyards, sheltered, interlinked,
of screens and arches, ornate plasterwork
around flat rectangles, pure mirrors set
to make a light show, endless flickering
reflected on the patterns of the walls.

No gargoyles spewing out their waste.
Here every drop's conserved
passed on by intricate machinery,
the rivulets, the water wheels,
feed countless outlets, always moving on...

The murmuring system never sleeps.
Clay pipes and filters form a skeleton
spreading the message to the outer limbs,
the gardens – fruit trees, flowers, herbs
packed in between the myrtle shrubs.

Within a massive geometric frame
of squares and circles, endless rows
the fountains play baroque accompaniment
as yellow   orange   red   explode
beneath that bright blue sky.

Significance is fluid. Purity.
The origin of life. The daily means
of cleansing, sanitising the latrine.
Prelude to prayer. And finally
a glimpse of paradise.

To Hell and Back

This story has a hero but he's not the usual sort
'Cos Abu's nearly forty, he's balding and he's short.
His family confront him because he smokes and drinks.
He tells his wife "I'm leaving you." Things can't get worse, he thinks.

From Turkey back to Syria he's slipping through the gate
To find a better, purer life, to serve Islamic State.
He knows he's not a fighter – "A desk job, that's for me."
"First you must do the training and then, perhaps, we'll see."

Film of a prisoner burnt alive. He knows that this is wrong.
They stare at him and start to think this weakling won't last long.
They tell him that he's heading for the front line in Iraq.
"I volunteered for admin"... but there is no way back.

There's martyrs who give everything, kids running to their death
But Abu has to take a break. He sits and gasps for breath.
The captain holds a suicide belt "Reach Paradise – for free"
Says Abu "Put it on yourself. You want that more than me."

He faces the commander. He's not prepared to kill:
"The prophet did not force his men to fight against their will."
Somehow he gets away with it. They want him out the way
So he's sent back behind the lines – he could die any day.

Then Abu's in a café, trying to save his life;
He goes online, and gets a call, a message from his wife.
It feels like a miracle, a time-out from the war
When for a moment he recalls the life he had before.

There's men who smuggle people out from under ISIS' eyes
So Abu's riding pillion, sweating, in disguise.
He's not equipped for action, his plans have come to grief
And when they cross the border he is shaking like a leaf.

Two figures sitting on a bench, a Turkish public park;
The birdsong and the sunshine, a rescue from the dark.
They talk for hours. His wife remarks "You're weak, like other men.
But Abu, I shall take you back. Just don't mess up again."

Odyssey

Hassan is doing well. Sure, he can see
the marches, vaguely knows civilians die.
Then teenage kids are tortured. That's not right.
He goes on demos, films them, claims the power
to post online. They grab him from his home
and break his arms in prison. Maybe fear

will change his mind. But then: "No need to fear.
Assad has heard about you. Wants to see
why rich kids' teacher should abuse his home.
You're safe. I cross my heart and hope to die."
So hopeful Hassan speaks his truth to power
and then, next day, he's back in prison, right?

Syria's not safe. Where do they do things right?
Where people have no need to live in fear?
Somehow the camera gives him added power,
furtively filming on a Turkish sea.
Three years adrift, then Calais. Mustn't die
must get himself to England – freedom's home.

He gets there, and it doesn't feel like home.
The poster "Breaking Point." He has no right
to money from the film. Yes, he could die
but he's the refugee, the extra. Fear
is in his job description. He can see
the white, the rich, the settled have the power.

And now there's Covid. No-one has the power
when a pandemic calls the shots. His home
is under threat, so Hassan goes to see
if he can help. Covid ward cleaner, right?
It's different and he's never known such fear.
A mongrel gang of mates; they all could die.

But still nothing is free. Before they die
these workers pay the NHS. It's power
gone mad. He grabs his phone, and shares his fear
with Johnson, everyone. This is his home
and how he's being treated isn't right.
Next day the rules are changed. It works. You see?

His hopes won't die. He wants to set up home
but those in power won't give up the right
to make him fear. He'll have to wait and see.

A Lesson from Auschwitz

Never again. We'll learn from this, we said.
Life is a rat race. I'm the toughest rat
was one survivor's message from the dead.
Edith, from Auschwitz, has a different take:
If you're all "me me me" you won't survive.
Her group's sustained by fantasy and cheek.
A beauty contest. Prize, a piece of bread.
Who's got the finest breasts? They all confer.
She wins the bread, divides it into five.
The death march moves them on from there. The weak
get left behind, or put aside and shot.
Edith's too frail. Her friends combine again, to make
a cradle of their arms, and carry her.
She shared. She loved. And that's why she's alive.

Syrian Feast

We're looking down at them. A drone, maybe,
or from a tower. But that's unlikely here.
Look at the edges of this shattered scene;
their walls in ruins, remnants from a past
before the madness when the whole world changed.

They are not looking up at us. They see
only their kids. Whatever else has gone
the end of Ramadan is not routine.
This, children, is the way we break our fast.

A neat rectangle. Mattresses obey
geometry; the mat is bright and clear
against the dismal rubble's standard grey.
A dozen dishes, carefully arranged,
bring order to this chaos. Life goes on.

The Lighthouse, Wolverhampton

The wind is up
the tides are treacherous
and no direction's safe.
That's when you need a beacon in the dark
a sign that you don't have to drown alone.

There's all sorts here.
Cinemas, galleries, café, meeting space.
And ragbag customers as well,
all kinds of jobs, retired, unemployed;
all ages, colours, genders, faiths
and some who aren't sure what they are.
Which is the point.
We're welcome, all of us
and that's why we keep coming here.
Unlock the mystery that Chubb contrived
and stroll across the cobbles, pass the time.
Escape the tyranny of solitary screens
and share a screening, celebrate a film.

It's not the smoothest.
People love this place
because it's not the smoothest. It has heart
and people who are glad to see you here
who know that social distancing
is temporary, not a fact of life.

The storm outside is gathering
and some accept the devil's estimate
of what we can afford.
To them, this friendly beam
is part nostalgia, part extravagance.
They won't mind watching, if it slowly dies.
So those who want to keep the light alive
must gather close, cling on to it
as if for dear, dear life.

Delroy's Path

It's Dudley, twenty twenty-five.
School leavers struggle to survive.
Pandemic's over, life's still tough
and platitudes are not enough.
The dream of full employment's gone
and no-one's taking youngsters on.
Quite what the future might be like
is hard to tell. Christ on a bike.
So Delroy's standing in the queue
preparing for his interview.

Stand-up, you say? I've seen your act
and we both know that it's a fact
black lads from here can make the grade.
I'll tell you how this game is played.
Most of your audience is white.
They won't know how to take you, right?
You mustn't scare them. Treat them nice.
In fact, if you take my advice
act dumber than you are. You make
the joke against yourself, to break
the ice. You need to calculate
which path to take. You watch and wait
and later, you may get the choice
to speak more freely, find your voice.
We've got experience. We can tell
who'll make the big time. You'll do well.

He nods, and saunters out the door.
He doesn't smash him to the floor.
He's just an oldie, decent chap
who doesn't know he's talking crap.
But Delroy's certain he won't win
apologising for his skin.
He won't seek out that winding track
which skirts around the fact he's black.
He'll fight his corner, stake his claim
'cos stop and search is not a game.
He'll do the jokes, he'll make 'em laugh
but no-one writes his epitaph.
Whether he sucks or he's a star
don't tell him where the limits are.

The Ballad of Tracy Rogers

You all know Tracy Rogers,
the child superstar
who grew up with the chorus
"That Tracy – she'll go far."

Her voice was clear as crystal,
blonde hair, a gorgeous smile.
If you're looking for an angel
she's flying, Texas style.

Her parents are behind her,
they're giving wise advice
and all the time they're drumming in
that golden rule – be nice.

Keep smiling as they watch you
be who you need to be;
thousands of girls watch Tracy
and think "she's just like me."

This isn't country any more,
the band, the smoke machines.
If you thought Tracy was a kid
just watch those dance routines.

Success creates a pressure
she can't afford to fail;
the online echo chamber
shunts stardom off the scale.

Reporters sniffing round her for
whatever they can find
but private stuff stays private
and it's gentle on her mind.

A local woman candidate
has plans to change the law
the right to an abortion
is one she would withdraw.

That's no surprise to Tracy
she's heard it all her life
but somehow, at this moment,
it cuts her like a knife.

A million of fans will hear her words.
This, maybe, is the hour
she gets to make things happen,
to exercise some power.

Her father and her managers
are smiling, almost laugh:
"Sure, go ahead, but you'll lose fans.
You'll cut your sales in half."

There's just one vote in her support,
her mother understands;
but Tracy's doing it anyway
her future's in her hands.

She learns the law of politics –
you fight, and then you lose.
But Tracy won't regret it 'cos
she's had the right to choose.

You can't believe the venom
controversy will bring.
That old familiar chorus
"Hey you! Shut up and sing."

Men talk of what they'd do to her
as if they had the choice;
the death threats are a megaphone
designed to drown her voice.

But Tracy's in the studio
her voice is doing fine;
she feels another album
coming down the line.

Those images inside her head,
she works to make them real;
imagines different stories
and the way that people feel.

Fitting the words to music
all day and late at night
and the closest thing to heaven
is when she gets it right.

Woke?

Me too. I get it now. Penelope –
don't laugh. I'm serious. Can't we begin
again? The way I was – that wasn't great.
Seduced by sirens, and a macho slave
to the one-eyed fury of competing males
who can't abide a stranger in the cave.
No self-control. That old calypso tune
of firmer flesh and younger, smoother skin.
Just fantasy, I know. I've put on weight,
lost hair. Skin's like a wrinkled prune.

You're looking good. But all those suitors… no
I've got no right to even ask. Forget
I mentioned it. Neat tapestry. I feel
I missed a lot because I chose to go.
Our son grew up, confronted puberty
without his dad. Same old. The father fails
because he's hatching up some cunning plan
out in the shed. Just storing up regret.
I know that you deserve a better deal
but I still am – I always was – your man.

Homeless at Christmas

"The foxes have holes, and the birds of the air
have nests; but the Son of Man hath not where
to lay his head." (Matthew 8.20)

A struggle from the start.
Bumping along a stony road,
knocking on doors, in winter.
This woman, apprehensive, looking out
explaining that she's really sorry but
her husband says she can't
let any vagrants in.

We have our homes, our castles,
keep them locked.
This was the promise, the reward
for which we worked so hard.
The homes for heroes.
Ladder, moving up
the signal of success.

Outside our walls, beneath our eyes
the sleeping bags, the dogs.
The paper cups.
Behind the plaintive voices, anxious looks
are endless tales of grief
of how one person, from a family
starting inside a house
ends up without a home.
In a shop doorway, these December nights
how lonely does it get?

Keep warm at Christmas.
Turn the heating up.
Be generous to your family –
the season to be jolly has arrived.
Why should you feel obligation, guilt?
You have done nothing wrong.

But as you move between
your kitchen, bathroom, bed
remember that you have these things
and count your lucky stars.

There and Back

Covid-19's no picnic;
there's a load of gruesome stuff.
What Rachel Rymar's facing
is definitely tough.

One toddler to look after
and now another's due.
At times like this it's family
that helps to pull you through.

Her mother would be glad to help
–   that's Yoshie, 63.
The only snag? She's miles away
in Washington DC.

She checks up on the websites
for stuff she needs to know;
there's nothing in the rules that says
she's not allowed to go.

Her plane touched down at Heathrow
and it's virtual arrest:
"So, madam, have you taken a
coronavirus test?"

When she said no they shook their heads.
It hit her like a smack.
"Your journey's non-essential.
You'll take the next plane back."

They took her to the ticket desk,
they booked her on a flight
and she was back in Washington.
Thank you, and good night.

She never spoke to Rachel;
the speed of it's absurd.
No pause for thought, enquiry,
–   just go, without a word.

OK, there's social distancing,
families split apart
but who was it decided on
a lockdown of the heart?

Somebody thinks we wanted this.
They did it in our name.
What happened to Yoshie Rymar
should make us die of shame.

Return to Work

It seemed so bright and clear.
Maggie had built her sewing shop
from scratch, recruited staff, got orders in
and heard that rhythm, felt the buzzing hum
of doing business well. Then lockdown came.
Furlough the workers, turn the key
and watch the clouds roll in.

But there's a gap.
No, not a gap. More like a hole.
A hole that is a mouth,
the rounded protest of an angry nurse
shouting at men who've made her work a war;
who'd urge her on, over the top again,
with kit that doesn't work.
Protection's what she needs and all she asks
but bloody promises are not the same.

So that's the hole, and Maggie is the peg.
The fit is perfect – spread the pattern out:
her skillset, and their need. They match.
At first she thinks she's doing this alone
but Facebook's teeming with The Love of Scrubs –
a teacher filling isolated hours,
a granny with an ancient Singer still,
a wardrobe mistress on a silent stage.
The hum comes back. They work to fill the hole,
to plug the gap, to give the cloud
a silver lining, loving and precise,
to wrap around the ones who guard
the fabric of our lives.

Short-term Investment

I am not here on holiday. This shift
is not a day-trip – selfie and move on.
Here in the ICU I work as long
as home-grown doctors, am exposed the same
but with more risk. I do have darker skin.

When my wife sees me off I see the fear
that's written on her face. If I get ill?
If I transmit infection to our son?
And if I die, who'll get the mortgage paid?
Will they be locked up? Shoved on to a plane?

My visa is extended for a year.
So, just enough to see this crisis through
and then we're back to normal, where I'm shed
like soiled PPE. Disposable.

Hippocrates at Wuhan

Li Wenliang said cases that he saw
reminded him of SARS. His chat group posts
warned colleagues to be careful what they wore.
Official antibodies, hostile hosts,
discerned a threat that had to be seen off.
"False comments" were the mark of something sick,
a virus needing treatment by the law.
He's bullied into silence, gets a cough,
a fever, hospital. But "nothing new"
according to the body politic.
His pregnant wife will see him die before
their second child is born. He's feeling rough,
but manages one final interview:
"For health, a single voice is not enough."

The other virus

The camera pans across Trafalgar Square.
It's empty. The abusers, we are told,
no longer walk among us. Then the twist –
if not out there, where has the violence gone?
Back down in here, within the flimsy walls
that can't contain it. Simmering inside
accumulated grievances: the crime
of workless poverty; of sex denied
and love witheld, of hopes and chances missed.
The court appearances, the frantic calls.
Contagion spreads, as teenage kids go spare,
enact the young's revenge against the old.
There's not the staffing, money, space or time
to ease the pressure. This goes on, and on.

Liberation

There always was that difference in age.
At fifty-five the Sheikh is in control
of Dubai and the UAE, alive
to power's subtleties, but why rule out
this princess raised in the Jordanian court?
Haya is smart, and twenty-nine years old.

Maybe a sixth wife stops him getting old.
The ideal couple for a global age,
celebrities at home in any court,
chat with the Queen at Ascot. Keep control
of money, power, deals. Nothing comes out
unless it's been approved. Plutocracy's alive

and well. For Princess Shamsa, being alive
meant Cambridge stablegirls, twenty years old,
with boyfriends. She attempted to get out
but then she vanished. Though police took an age
they found no trace. Someone was in control,
whisked her away. It never got to court.

Next up, Latifa, skydiver. She's caught
aboard a yacht, near India. Scarcely alive,
they dragged her to the home she's fled. Control
stays in Dubai; it's men on women, old
on young, no change. The tyranny of age
that locks the doors, won't let the story out.

Latifa made her plans, and smuggled out
a video diary. Even though she's caught
this rebel daughter of the snapchat age
can warn her step-mum, help to keep alive
the dream of freedom. Haya's not too old
to see a life beyond the sheikh's control

in London. With an effort, she'll control
the tremors as she takes her children out
and asks for custody. Her husband's told
his wealth can't buy the verdict of this court.
He writes a poem – "whether you're alive
or dead I do not care" – burning with rage

that he has lost control. This English court
rubs out possession, keeps her hopes alive.
Dubai is sprayed with gold. It's still a cage.

Freedom Fighter

i.m. Ernesto Cardenal (1925-2020),
Nicaraguan poet and priest

In 1983 the Pope's in town
to greet the smiling rebels who lay claim
to independence. Now Somoza's gone
their Nicaragua can at last be free.
The Pontiff smiles at each of them, bar one;
Ernesto is the priest who crossed the line
that separates the church from politics.
What line? He is a poet, couldn't see
the tidy boundaries men in power lay down.
God, love, his people. They are all the same.
Ortega comes to power, gets his fix,
gets hooked. He can't see why he should resign.
At 95, it breaks Ernesto's heart
to watch his country being torn apart.

Leavers

So many different motives, dreams combined:
Great Britain, and the confidence that's lost;
the London bubble where the money went;
smug old Etonians and austerity;
the NHS, the foreigners. Begin
the fightback now, to claim their place.
This time, for once, they know each vote will count.

Euphoria in Sunderland. They win!
A massive turnout: fifty-two per cent.
That's seventeen million – a huge amount.
But four years later anyone can see
they were just digits on a database,
not taking back control but left behind.
Their votes were cancelled. They were double-crossed.

Armour

It drives them mad, my shiny carapace.
My smirk on screen, my educated vowels,
easing their way through reasoned argument.
If you've a grudge against smug southerners,
you'd take the surface evidence as proof
that I am guilty; you'd assume
that I must think myself superior.

You would not see how I got into this.
The senior colleague in a corridor
who stopped me, bullied, harassed me –
You have to do this for the rest of us.
Promotion not as appetite for power
but simply to avoid embarrassment.
You really think I could? Well, if I must...

I nursed my dad when he was sad and old
although he'd left me, twice. At seventeen
I'm stuck in London, he's off to New York.
No way I'm going back to mum – too proud.
So I stay put, alone and hardening.
Odd jobs in factories, pulling pints.
A cleaner on the ferries, mopping sick.

Not a high flier. Failed eleven plus.
The sec mod bullies sought me out,
echoed the darker whispers in my head
that I was rubbish. Four years earlier
our dad walked out on all of us.
A small, cramped house. The pocket money shrank.
On free school meals. The cats put down.

And now I walk these corridors
with serious intent, against the odds,
to govern, have a say in what comes next.
There's flak and plotting, social media storms,
the sewage tide of rumour, leak and threat
but that's the territory. People look up to me
expect me to be strong. That's what I'll be.

Step back

into the ironmonger's shop
over the lines of dusty boards
to where a honeycomb of pigeonholes
store fading entries from a time

when E.C.Davies the proprietor
wearily, formally requests
the payment of a year-old debt

when British Petroleum sends an invoice out
for nine pounds, fourteen shillings, seven pence
from Silk Street, Eccles, Manchester

when Mr. Davies, candidate
asks his constituents to vote once more
for Progress and Efficiency

when Wilmots offer steel water butts,
the "Palace" coop, the medium gauge pig fence
and a rat trap from the "Night Club" range.

Written at the Poetry Pharmacy, Bishops Castle

Pick-me-up:
a celebration of Fats Waller

The opening bars are irresistible,
that piano brushing up against my hand
an eager puppy looking for a stroke.
His rich, warm voice, the chuckle breaking in,
the smart ad libs. Don't let it bother you
he says. To give up hope would be a sin
and here comes consolation, bang on cue.
That "when somebody thinks you're wonderful"
excitement, just imagine the surprise
of loving, being loved. The endless joke
that you can write yourself a letter, and
believe that everything will be OK.
It might sound sentimental, but it's wise
and makes me smile. I'm fit to face the day.

Notes on Rescue from the Dark

p9. *Rescue*

Where do poems come from? Michael Longley's response was "If I knew that, I'd go there." Mine's much more prosaic: *The Guardian*. That's been my paper for as long as I can remember; and I do mean paper. The online operation is brilliant, but it isn't the same.

Here the original impetus was that iconic photo, of the huge black man carrying a white protestor. But the documentary details of his argument – of why exactly he was doing this – were taken from subsequent reports (15-16.6.20).

This poem was one of the one-a-day sequence of sonnets that I wrote and posted during the first fourteen weeks of lockdown, subsequently collected as "Turning Off the News." (TOTN)

p10. *Betrayal*

This was based on a *Guardian* profile of a young doctor, and again it's the length and detail which are important. You could predict that she'd feel exhaustion and justified fear, but what struck me was the degree of guilt – she had symptoms, so she had to stay off work, but so did her flatmates. That's how "this bastard" virus infiltrates past defences, right to the heart.

p12. *Dover Beach, June 2016*

I wrote this poem in the week before the Brexit vote. We didn't know what the result would be, but we knew how and why Jo Cox was killed.

Matthew Arnold's poem "Dover Beach" was published in 1867. I've echoed its atmosphere, of unease following a loss of certainty, but also there are direct echoes, in lines 1, 16, 17 and 31.

p14. A chat with Clem in 1951
Clement Attlee led the Labour government after the Second World War, and there has been a massive change in how he is seen. For years he was thought of as a dull, pedestrian figure, a nonentity in Churchill's shadow. Looking now at what his government achieved between 1945-51, he's an inspiration to many Labour supporters, and in my imaginary conversation with him there are contrasts and parallels with today's politics.

p16. Winter
This is based on a Brueghel picture, *The Hunters in the Snow*, 1565, and is one of a sequence of sonnets I have written, each based on a Breughel painting. His paintings are over four hundred years old, but vital with endless detail, humming with life.

p17. Ecosystem
If you were asked to list damaging consequences of pollution, you wouldn't come up with a rising death rate among vultures. But there are parts of Pakistan where it's been disastrous.

p18. Special Offer
This poem won the *Scottish Huntington's Disease* poetry competition in 2018. I had no previous knowledge of the disease, so it was only through research for the poem that I grasped quite how insidious and damaging its effects can be.

p19. Testimony
I've been fascinated and appalled by the revelations that have followed the Grenfell fire. (There've been regular reports in *The Guardian*, but if you want to explore in more detail, check out *The Grenfell Tower Enquiry* podcast, on bbc sounds.) Most of the

people employed by cladding and building firms have been anxious to play pass the parcel with blame, but I was struck by a different tone in the evidence of John Hoban. A building control surveyor, he was appalled by what had happened, and clear about how the staffing of his workplace had contributed to that. (*Guardian*, 2.10.20)

p20. *Fit for Purpose?*
The immediate response to the Grenfell fire in June 2017 was that a short-sighted, insensitive council had ignored the concerns and safety of its residents. In June 2018 this view was challenged by Andrew O'Hagan, in a long, influential article for the *LRB*, which argued that the council members had been misunderstood, and that resident activists had been misguided. The evidence which has emerged from the Grenfell enquiry powerfully supports the original, immediate response.

p22. *Frances at Nashoba*
I discovered Frances Wright and Nashoba at New Lanark in 2013, on a trip to Edinburgh and Glasgow. New Lanark was the base for the factory owner and social reformer Robert Owen (1771-1858), who – like Frances Wright – attempted to create a Utopian society in America.

p24. *On the Edge*
This poem was commended in the *Welshpool* poetry competition (Theme: Jewel) of 2018. On holiday in Whitby, I'd read about the fashion for Whitby jet, massively stimulated by the enthusiasm for it shown by the mourning Queen Victoria.

p26. *Living in Limbo*
When I wrote this poem, the Kurdish Iranian Behrouz Boochani was still incarcerated at Manu Island. (August 2019). He's since

been released to freedom in New Zealand and a life as a successful author. This does not apply to other victims of the Australian immigration system, and our government remains eager to replicate their success, hunting for something – an island, a ship – where unwanted migrants can be dumped out of sight.

p28. The Ballad of Paulette Wilson
Paulette Wilson was the first of the Windrush cases to be reported, in articles by Amelia Gentleman, who had been alerted by the Wolverhampton Refugee and Migrant Centre. I'm proud to have been one of the local poets involved in the benefit event to which the poem refers. Paulette has died, but Windrush remains a scandal, as does the deliberate failure to learn its lessons.

p30. The Idea of the Garden
Katherine Swift is the author of *The Morville Hours*, a record of the wonderful garden she has created, which is four miles down the road from my home. This poem was written for a celebration of the Summer Solstice in 2018, held at Morville, which Katherine and I organised.

p32. Funny Girl
The impetus for this poem was provided by a book-signing at the much-missed Wenlock Books. In the summer of 2004 Jacky Fleming came to promote her book *Demented*, and this poem describes her encounter with a customer.

p34. A Class Act
In 2019 the artist Steve McQueen organised the project *Year Three*. Each of 76,000 London pupils, aged 7-8, was involved in a class photo at their school. Then they came into Tate Britain to see the photos, and take part in activities.

p35. Oaks
This was written at Ercall, near Telford, on a workshop run by
Paul Evans, one of the writers of *The Guardian*'s Country Diary.

p36. Dominic Cummings Explains:
In spring 2021 everybody knows about Dominic Cummings'
drive to Durham, because it was one of the key events of 2020.
In later years, however, readers may need to be aware of the
following details:

In 2020 Dominic Cummings, the mastermind behind the vote to
Leave, was Boris Johnson's most powerful adviser. When his wife
exhibited Covid symptoms, he drove her and their son up to
Durham, and then had a day-trip to Barnard Castle, to test that
his eyesight was good enough to drive back down to London.
All of this was in defiance of government advice, but Johnson
refused to sack him, and Cummings insisted on holding his own
press conference to explain himself. This poem is based on
detailed accounts of that event.

The subtitle – "how we brought the symptoms…" – acknowledges
Browning's poem "How we brought the good news from Ghent
to Aix", which provides the model for the rhythm and rhyme-
scheme.

p38. Clocking Off
This poem was based on a *Guardian* article, and was included in
the *Bread and Roses* anthology, published by Culture Matters,
2020.

p40. Sir Arthur Conan Doyle
The writer Laura Spinney has been prolific during the pandemic,
because of the detailed research which went into *Pale Rider*, her

history of the Spanish Flu. This current pandemic has often been described as "unprecedented", but there are certainly parallels from which we can learn. This first appeared in TOTN.

p41. Fatal Attraction
This is also featured in the TOTN sequence. It's based on one of those quirky human stories which *The Guardian* cherishes more affectionately than any other paper (March 2020).

p42. Man to Man
This was written for an online course in response to a prompt from Leah Umansky, who gave us a Cynthia Manick poem, *Things I will tell my children about destiny*. "We are living in some dark times right now. What are some things you would tell the future generations about their destiny?" I wrote about an imaginary conversation with my son, though it might yet happen.

p43. Mentor
This poem makes use of a *Guardian* profile of the country singer Kacey Musgraves. As an ex-teacher, I'm impressed by an example of really smart education, finding the right route to stimulate a young talent.

p44. Working with Water
This poem describes the irrigation arrangements at the Generalife, the gardens which are part of the Alhambra complex at Granada. It was written for a competition whose central theme was Water; it came nowhere.

p46. To Hell and Back
The story of this poem was provided by a *Guardian* article in April 2016.

p48. Odyssey
I encountered the amazing story of Hassan Akkad in two separate contexts. (1) I was compiling a pamphlet of poems about migration, and he was one of the migrants featured in *Exodus*, a three-part TV documentary in which migrants were given cameras with which to record their journeys (shown on BBC 2 in July 2016). (2) He then reappeared, as a hospital worker filming a protest to government ministers, about the lack of protection during the pandemic. (*Observer* 2.8.20)

p50. A Lesson from Auschwitz
This was based on a TV documentary, from February 2020.

p51. Syrian Feast
My affection for *The Guardian* isn't based on their editorial stance – I hardly ever read their leader columns. What I like is the detail with which they report, and their willingness to present a range of views in their comment pages. But I also love their respect for good photography – some of their themed displays at the heart of the paper are just brilliant. The particular aerial photo on which this poem is based covered the entire double-page spread.

p52. The Lighthouse, Wolverhampton
In summer 2020 Creative Black Country commissioned a project to encourage the writing of poems about various areas in the Black Country. This was my submission for the Wolverhampton leg, based on the community arts centre, The Lighthouse, which was once the site of the the locksmiths Chubb.

p54. Delroy's Path
Another submission for the *Stay Up Your Own End* project, run by the wonderful collective, Poet, Prattlers and Pandemonialists. This was for the Dudley leg, based on the early career of Lenny Henry.

p56. *The Ballad of Tracy Rogers*
Tracy is my own invention, but she owes a debt to parts of the career of Taylor Swift, as recorded in *Miss Americana* (Netflix).

p59. *Woke?*
This is my contemporary twist on the ending of *The Odyssey*, which I wrote for a pamphlet entitled *Men Too: myths of masculinity*.

p60. *Homeless at Christmas*
This was written at short notice for a friend, who was collecting poems about homelessness at Christmas. I have always loved responding to a particular stimulus and close deadline – for me it always gets the poetic juices flowing.

p62. *There and Back*
Long before it became a lazy way to describe a slow song, a ballad was a tight, tough story told in rhyming verse. It was one way for oral communities to preserve their history, and I love rediscovering that power in performance. I've always loved them, from hearing my mum recite Sir Patrick Spens, to listening to Marty Robbins' Gunfighter Ballads. This, the fourth ballad in this collection, is again based on a *Guardian* article. It came third in the Crewe Writers competition, 2020.

p64. *Return to Work*
A familiar combination of two factors – a *Guardian* article about the responses to the shortage of PPE, and a competition calling for poems in support of the NHS. Like *Betrayal* (page 10), this poem wasn't among the hundred poems selected for the anthology. But keep reading…

p65. *Short-term Investment*
This was one of the sonnets in TOTN, but it also came second in

the *Beyond the Storm* poetry competition, held in the summer of 2020 in support of the NHS. There were 2,300 poems entered, all of them read and judged for free by Andrew MacMillan.

The poem was very closely based on a letter in *The Guardian* from Dr. Mohammad Elshamy, of Preston. (14.4.20).
He detailed his conditions of work, his wife's concern for their family's future, and his plea for more security and support.

p66. *Hippocrates at Wuhan*
As the pandemic developed, the WHO and China worked hard to maintain an impression of collaboration and transparency. In the early stages, however, the Chinese bureaucracy reverted to type – secretive and punitive. So the first casualties were medical professionals who took huge risks to try to keep their patients and their colleagues safe. I find Li Wenliang's final words all the more moving because they're so restrained.

p67. *The other virus*
"Not now, while this crisis is on…" There are so many things which can't be dealt with while the pandemic is at its height, but which are nonetheless festering, and getting worse. Domestic violence is one, on a long list.

p68. *Liberation*
This is a complex family story, where different parts emerged at different times. I ended up with a bulging file of "Dubai Divorce" cuttings, but the most potent source was a BBC 2 documentary, *The Mystery of the Missing Princess* (shown in December 2018). This included a video diary which Latifa recorded in case her attempted escape failed. Since I wrote this poem there has been a revival of the Latifa story, with news reports of messages from her appealing for help in February 2021.

p70. Freedom Fighter
Another of the sonnets in TOTN. This poem is based on a
Guardian obituary (12.5.20).
For me there's also a family connection. My daughter Hilary wrote
an A level history study about Nicaragua more than twenty years
ago, and ever since she's been deeply involved in the country's
past, present and future. The betrayal of the Sandinista revolution
is one of the great tragedies of the twentieth century.

p71. Leavers
Write a poem that's critical of the Brexit process, and you'll be
branded as a Remoaner who can't stand to lose. In the year when
I joined the Labour Party, I canvassed for them at four different
levels of representation (local, county, national, European) and
lost every one. I can cope with losing. What annoys me about the
Brexit vote is not that it went the wrong way, but that it was an
illusory choice promoted by a fraudulent campaign. Thanks to
widely distributed failures of nerve, imagination and morality,
we are now facing a future which hardly anyone wants. And that
includes many Leavers.

p72. Armour
This was based on a *Guardian* profile of Emily Thornberry, Labour
MP and current member of the shadow cabinet. I was fascinated
by the distance it described, between the surface image and the
inner reality.

p74. Step back
On Bishops Castle high street, there is an old ironmonger's which
Deb Alma and Jim Sheard have taken over and transformed into
a Poetry Pharmacy. (There is no connection with the William
Sieghart poetry anthology). If you want more information, and
some stunning photos, Google "poetry pharmacy bishops castle."

I went to a workshop there soon after this transformation occurred, and this poem was a result.

p75. Pick-me-up

In my TOTN sequence, there was much criticism of the political incompetence which hampered our response to the pandemic, but I didn't want to end the series mired in gloom. Despite the circumstances, I wanted to end on a note of hope and joy. So let's hear it for – Mr. Fats Waller.